P9-CEA-982

Translated from the Swedish by Clare James

Photo assistant: Håkan Agnsäter

Editor: Per Wivall

Design: Bo Berling

A Merloyd Lawrence Book
Published by Delacorte Press
Bantam Doubleday Dell Publishing Group, Inc.
1540 Broadway
New York, NY 10036

Originally published in Sweden under the title
Vi ska få ett syskon by Bonnier Alba, Stockholm

Photographs copyright © 1993 by Lennart Nilsson
Text copyright © 1993 by Lena Katarina Swanberg
English translation copyright © 1994 by Dell Publishing Company, Inc.
All rights reserved

Library of Congress Cataloging-in-Publication Data
Nilsson, Lennart, 1922-
[Vi ska få ett syskon. English]
How was I born? / Lennart Nilsson, Lena Katarina Swanberg
[translated from the Swedish by Clare James].
p. cm.
ISBN 0-385-31357-8
1. Pregnancy—Pictorial works—Juvenile literature.
2. Childbirth—Pictorial works—Juvenile literature.
[1. Childbirth.   2. Pregnancy.   3. Brothers and sisters.]
I. Swanberg, Lena Katarina.   II. Title.
RG525.5.N5413   1994
612.6'3—dc20
94-11908
CIP
AC

Published simultaneously in Canada
November 1994

10 9 8 7 6 5 4 3 2 1

Primted in Spain by Artes Graficas Toledo, S.A.
D.L.TO:617-1994

Lennart Nilsson   Lena Katarina Swanberg

How Was I Born?

*My name is Mary. My big brother is called
John and he's six and a half. Thomas is our baby
brother. This is the story of how he was born.
I was born this way too!*

A Merloyd Lawrence Book

Delacorte Press

My mom is called Sally. She's happy and sometimes wears glasses. She's a nurse. Daddy is called Pete. He wears a suit when he's working, but not when he's home. Then he wears a sweater. His sweater smells nice. But not his suit—suits smell like banks.

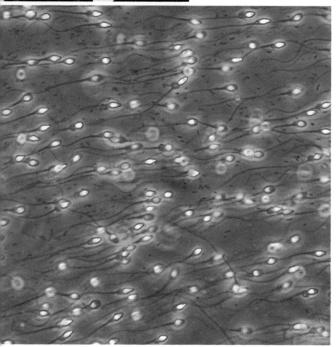

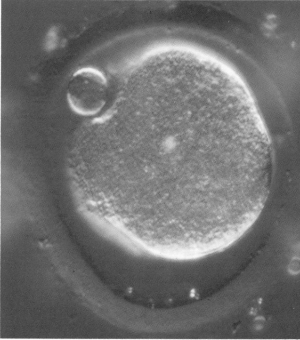

Inside the mother's belly are tiny eggs.* In the father's testicles are sperm, which are even smaller. For a new baby to start growing, an egg and a sperm have to meet. They do this when the mother and father have intercourse. This means that the father puts his penis inside the mother's vagina and many sperm come out through his penis.

Only one egg at a time is waiting inside the mother's belly. But all

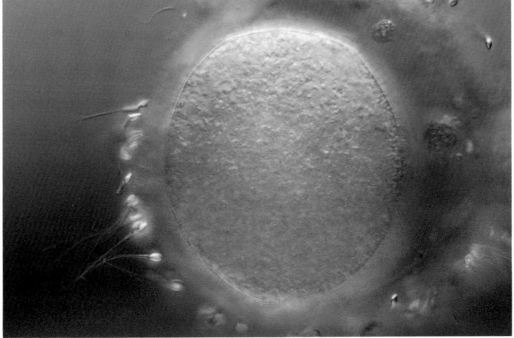

the sperm race to get to the egg first. They swim by waggling their small tails as fast as they can. When the first sperm arrives, it hurries to dig its way into the egg. Once this happens, no other sperm can get into the egg. Now a baby starts growing inside the mother.

But no one knows that yet—not even the mother and father.

* Note to parents: Younger children may be satisfied with Mary's story (in italics). The explanations (in roman type) can be read to, or by, the older child.

I remember exactly when Mom told us we had a brother or sister on the way. It wasn't just an ordinary day. I've never seen Daddy jump for joy before. Grown-ups don't usually jump up and down, except if they've got sweat suits on. We all jumped up and down. We were so happy! I wanted us all to fly up onto the roof of the house. That's how happy I was. John wanted to jump right up the chimney. Daddy said that having three children was heaven on earth. He jumped highest, because he has the longest legs.

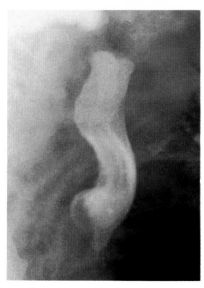

3 weeks, 1½ mm, 1/16 inch

*A*t first I wanted the baby to come right away. It's no fun just waiting
around. But Mom said the baby'd be born in the fall. It won't be ready until
then, she said. I got mad when Mom said that, because it was only winter.
Then comes spring, then it's summer and my birthday . . . and it's ages *till my
birthday!* But it's even longer *till the baby comes.*

Never mind about the baby, I said to Mom—maybe it's just going to be a
turtle or something. Then we went out and played in the snow and threw
snowballs, which was really fun!

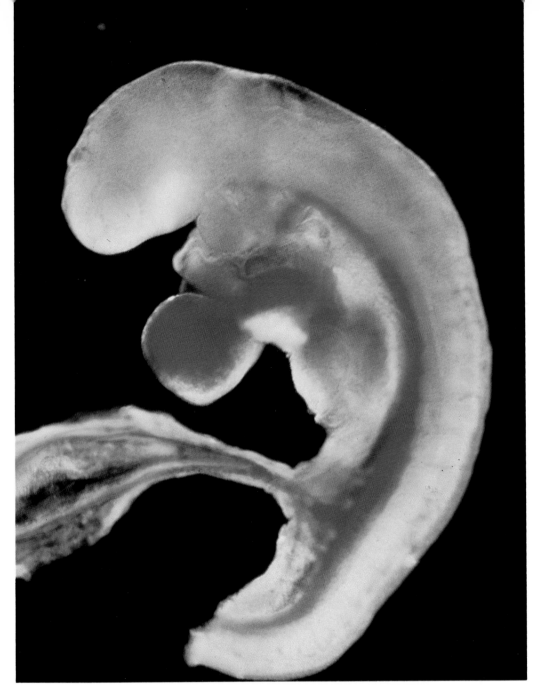

4 weeks, 6 mm, ¼ inch

In this picture, the baby is four weeks old. In real life it isn't nearly so big. It's really only the size of your little fingernail. You can see the baby's backbone, head, and heart. But it has no legs or arms, and no eyes or ears either. A baby that hasn't been born yet is called a fetus.

An ant is tiny too. It's funny that there's room for six legs on it anyway. John dares to hold an ant. I don't want to, because once an ant bit me. It got into my sock with three pine needles and a little stone. But only the ant hurt. There was a red mark where it bit me.

John's never been bitten. Only me.

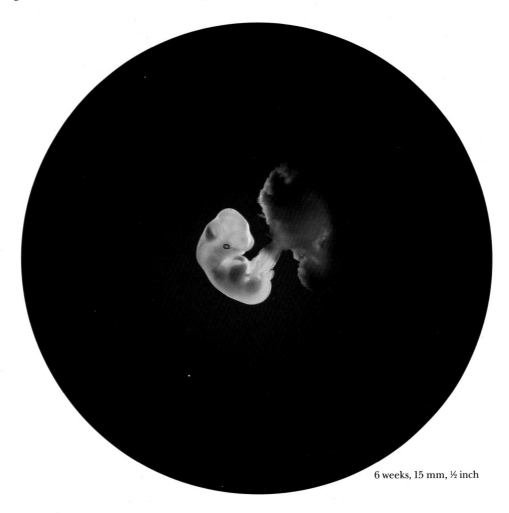

6 weeks, 15 mm, ½ inch

After six or seven weeks, the baby's arms, hands, and feet start to show. You can see the eyes as well.

Now the mother knows she's expecting a baby. But you can't see anything from the outside. The baby is hidden inside the mother's belly, and it's as small as an ant. The baby lies in a little room of its own, called the uterus.

*We've got a yard outside our house.
Raspberries and apples and grass grow
there. When it was spring, Daddy and John
planted seeds in pots. Some are going to be
tomatoes and some are going to be flowers.*

*I wonder if you sowed a boy seed or a girl
seed in Mom's tummy, John said to Daddy.
It's silly that the seeds are all mixed up.
Then you don't know what kind it's going
to be. Seed packets with pictures on them
are better.*

The baby in the picture is about six weeks old. It has plenty of room inside the mother's belly, since the baby's not much bigger than the bean John's holding. Although it's so small, the baby can move. Sometimes it even hiccups a bit.

It's snug and warm inside the mother's body. So the baby never gets cold while it's lying there and growing.

6 weeks, 15 mm, ½ inch

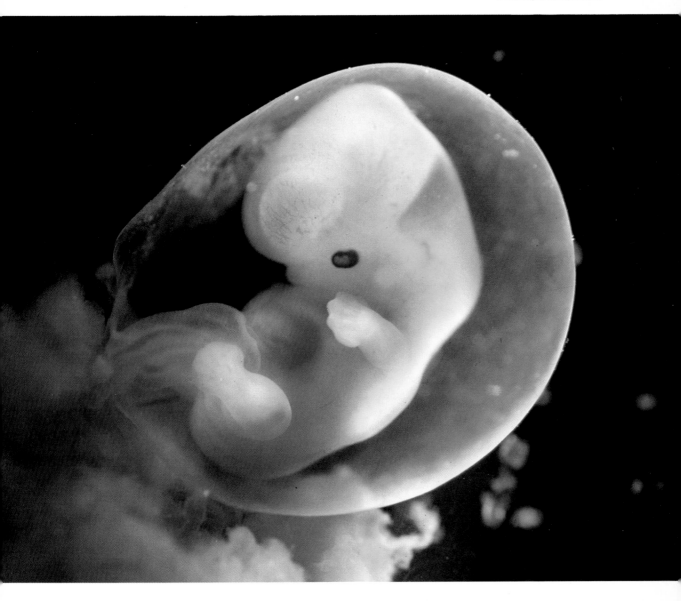

I'm awfully thirsty. I've run five times around our house and not stopped once. I don't really like apple juice. I like cranberry. But we've run out. That's why I had to run till I got so thirsty that I didn't notice the apple taste.

I know another trick for drinking juice. You hold the glass with both hands. Then you can't see the color. You drink through the straw, and it almost tastes like cranberry in your mouth.

Striped straws are my favorite.

All the food the baby needs before it is born comes through the umbilical cord. One end is attached to the uterus inside the mother's belly. The other end is attached to the baby, right where the belly button, called the navel, will be later. So it's important for a mother to eat good food when she's expecting a baby, because then the baby is well fed too. The cord is long so that the baby can move around.

6—7 weeks, 20 mm, ¾ inch

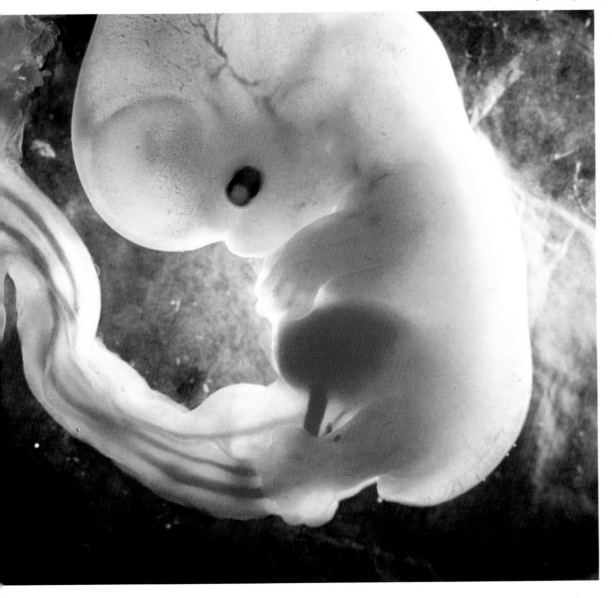

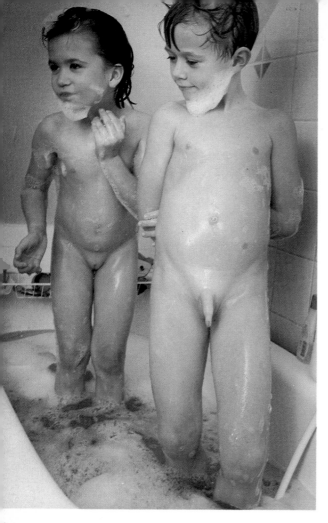

*S*ometimes when John and I are in the tub, we have a bubble bath. We play that we've got white beards, and we make hats out of the bubbles too. We pretend we're old, and walk around in the tub till we fall over.

Bubble baths are much more fun than just washing. In some bubble baths you can't have soap, because then all the bubbles pop.

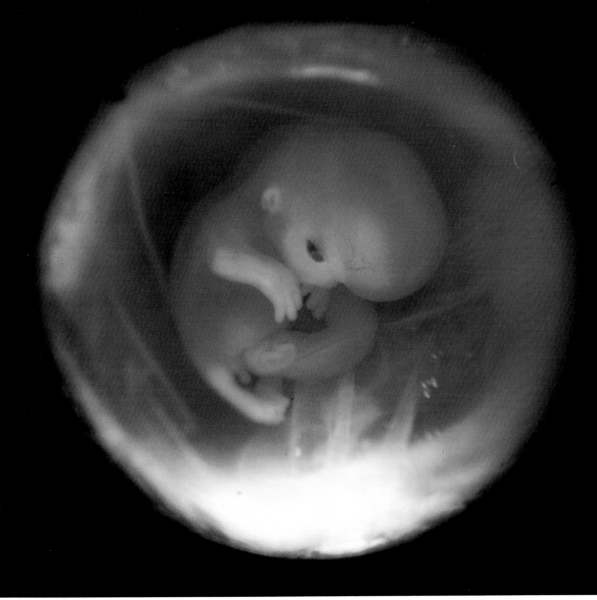

8 weeks, 25 mm, 1 inch

The sperm decides whether the baby will be a girl or a boy. That's because there are girl sperm and boy sperm, but only one kind of egg. When the baby is just beginning to grow inside the mother, you can't see any difference between a boy baby and a girl baby. After a while girls get a vagina and boys a penis. Doctors can find out whether it's a boy or a girl long before the baby is born. But many families would rather be surprised.

I have a friend named José. He's in the same preschool as me. We joke a lot together. We really get the giggles.

José has brown eyes, black hair, and brown skin. So do his mom and dad. I have brown eyes, brown hair, and light skin, like my mother. But Daddy has black hair, and John's is almost white.

In the summer I get nearly as brown as José. But my hair gets lighter than it is now. It changes in the sun.

A child always looks like both the father the sperm came from and the mother the egg came from. This is because the genes, which decide the color of the skin, eyes, and hair, and many other things, are inside both the sperm and the egg.

If a child is adopted it may not look like its adoptive parents, but it will act like them because mothers and fathers teach their child their language, their habits, and the way they live.

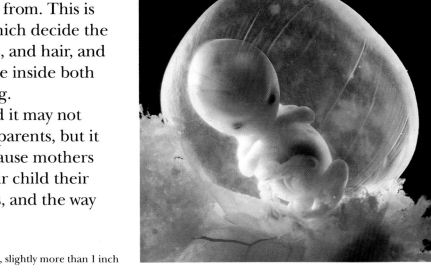

9 weeks, 30 mm, slightly more than 1 inch

The baby is peaceful and very comfortable inside the uterus, deep inside the mother's belly. At first the uterus is only as big as a pear, but it gets bigger as the baby grows. The walls are soft and the baby swims in water that is as warm as the skin on your own warm tummy.

The water is a little salty, and is called amniotic fluid. This water protects the baby in case the mother gets a hard bump on her belly. It also stretches out the uterus to make it easier for the baby to move around. The bigger the baby gets, the more water there is around it. When the baby is about to be born, there is about as much water as in a quart milk container.

You can see that the baby isn't ready to be born yet. But the hands now have tiny fingers and the feet tiny toes. Ears are beginning to grow too.

10—11 weeks, 35 mm, about 1⅓ inch (from head to buttocks)

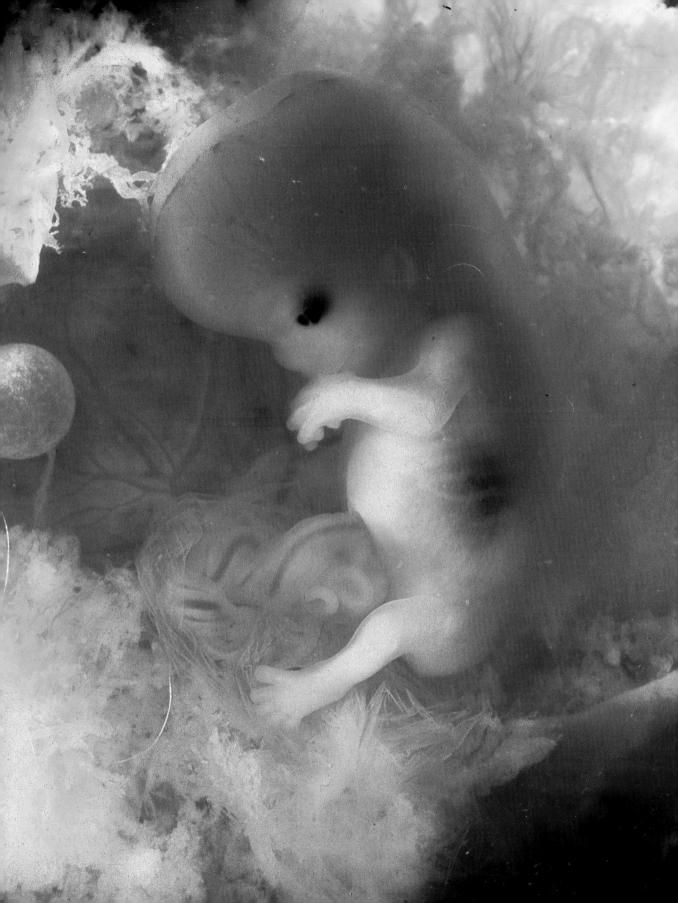

I went with Mom to see her doctor. The doctor made sure that both Mom and the baby in her tummy are healthy. They let me see our baby on the TV, although it's inside her tummy.

I thought the picture was fuzzy. I couldn't see whether it was a little sister or brother. But I could tell it was sucking its thumb.

not quite 4 months, 13 cm, 5 inches

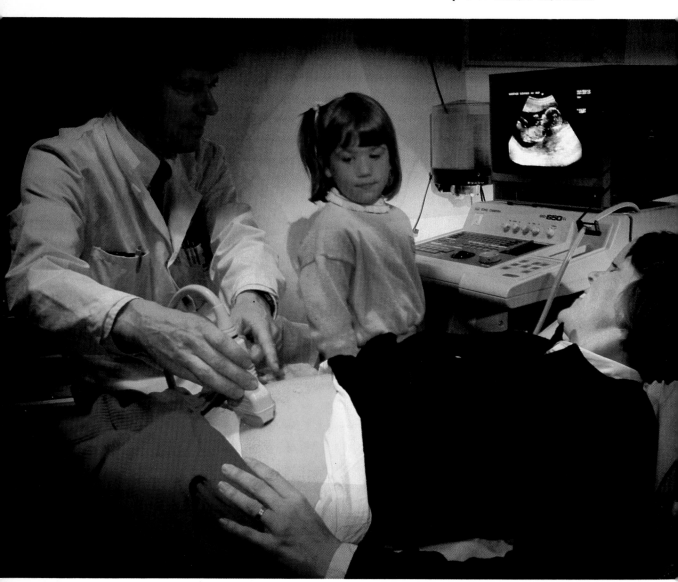

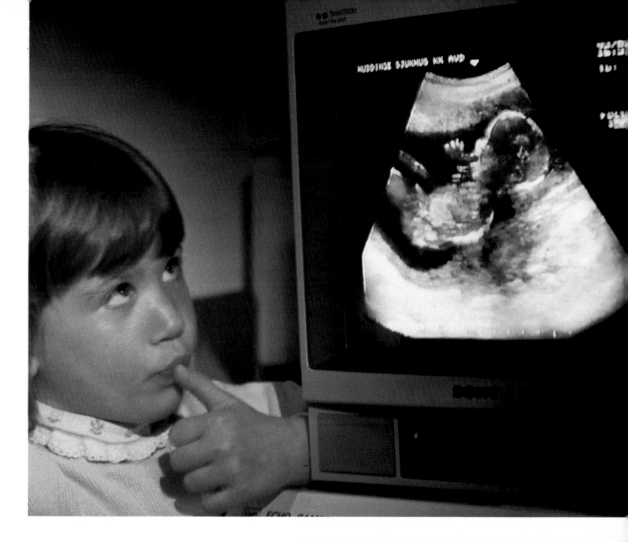

When the doctor wants to see how the baby is getting on inside the mother, he uses an ultrasound machine. It is like a TV screen. You can see the head and the arms and legs. If the mother is expecting twins, you can see that too.

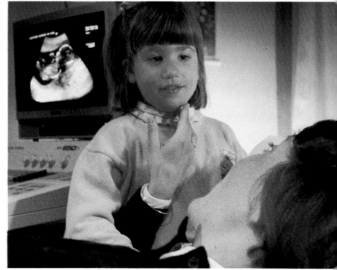

The doctor rubs oil on the mother's belly, to make it slippery. The baby comes on the screen when the tube called a transmitter slides over the mother's skin.

*J*ohn's so good at climbing. He dares to climb really high. When we're out playing on the jungle gym, he's almost always at the top. Or else he hangs upside down.

I'm good at climbing too. But I like swinging most, because my head likes being the right way up and my feet like pointing down. I don't see what's nice about being the other way around.

This baby's bones aren't ready yet. In the picture, you can see that the leg bones need to go on growing, so that they reach all the way from the knee down to the foot.

Before it is born, a baby has much softer bones than those in children who can already climb and run. Even the head is slightly soft; otherwise it might be too tight a squeeze when the baby is born.

After the baby is born, its bones get harder and stronger.

*W*hile we were waiting for the baby I thought a lot about it. When Daddy tucked me in at night I felt sorry for the baby, because no one tucked him in. He doesn't even have any toys in there, I said to Daddy. And no one sings lullabies to him either.

   Daddy says that the baby certainly does hear lullabies. They sound soft and quiet through the walls of the tummy. I thought that was good, because I sometimes wondered if the baby felt lonely.

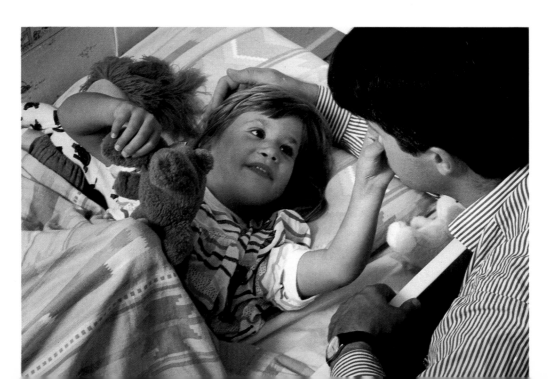

4½ months, 21 cm, slightly more than 8 inches

It's never really too quiet where the baby is, in the mother's belly.
There, in the soft, warm darkness, the baby hears bubbling noises
from the mother's stomach when she's been eating, and the gentle
thumping of her heart. Sometimes it can also hear voices through the
wall of the belly, and also music that is played up close.

When the mother walks back and forth, the baby floats gently and
is rocked to sleep, as if in a cradle.

I've decided something important. I'm going to give our new baby my old pacifiers. All of them. First I thought of giving them to Daddy. He said he really wished for them for his birthday. So I asked him which came first, his birthday or the baby's. Daddy said the baby would come much, much later.

I decided to give them to the baby anyway.

I chose some wrapping paper with Mickey Mouse on it and made a pretty package with tape and ribbon.

5 months, 25 cm, 9¾ inches

Inside the mother's belly, the baby gets plenty of food through the umbilical cord. But as soon as it's born, it has to be able to suck on the mother's breasts to get fed.

That's why the baby practices sucking while it's still inside. It waves its hands, and every time it happens to touch its mouth, the mouth starts sucking by itself. It's called the sucking reflex. The baby sucks without anyone teaching it how.

When it gets really warm outside, then it's my birthday. I always have my party outdoors. This time we had a cake with candy on top. I helped make it.

The good thing about my birthday is that it's right at the beginning of summer. Then you can play outside in the sun, and you can roll over in the grass when you laugh.

John had a tie on and I was wearing my best dress with the big collar. And John had to help me with some of the presents, because I got so many. Then we had the funniest race, with our feet in garbage bags.

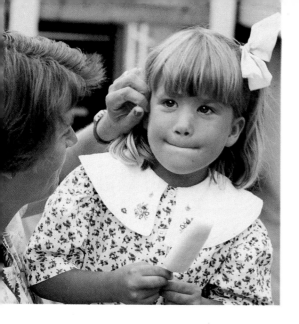

Blowing real balloons is terribly hard. Soap bubbles are much easier and they are so pretty when they fly away.

When they burst they go pop, but you can hardly hear it. Then there's a tiny wet spot where the bubble landed. It doesn't matter, even if you have your best clothes on.

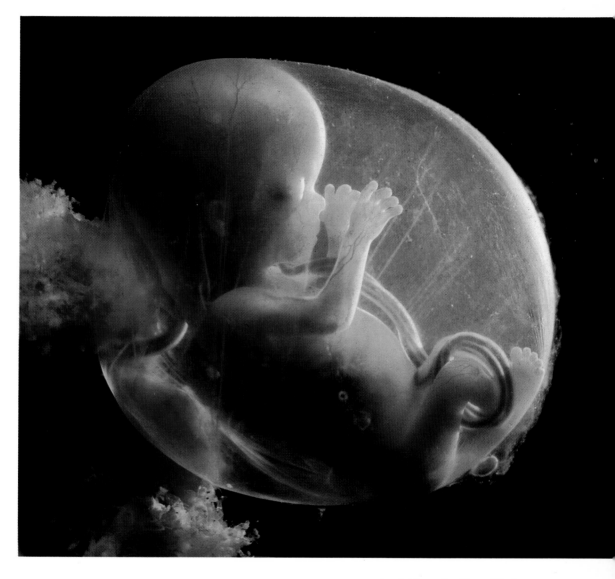

not quite 4 months, 13 cm, 5 inches

Inside the mother's belly, in the uterus, the baby lies in a strong
bubble called the amniotic sac, which is filled with amniotic fluid.
When the baby is about to be born, the sac bursts and all the fluid
runs out. The sac is very strong, like a balloon filled with water. Sometimes the doctor has to help break it so that the baby can come out.

But it's not time yet. It takes forty weeks—about nine months—
before a baby is quite ready to be born.

*T*he baby's kicking! Both John and I felt it ourselves with our hands! The foot felt just like a little bump, and you could see Mom's tummy move too. The foot even moved when we pressed it a bit. John and Mom and I tried to guess where the baby would kick next time.

*A*fter a while the bump came back in a new place, but never where we put our fingers.

Sometimes the whole of Mom's tummy was going up and down all over the place, the baby was moving so much inside. And once when I put my ear on Mom's tummy the baby boxed me on the cheek!

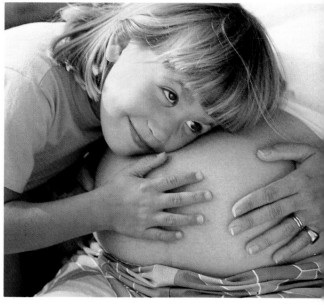

*J*ohn had the idea of putting a glass of juice on Mom's tummy and seeing how hard the baby could kick. It was exciting. We waited and waited.

5½ months, 30 cm, 11¾ inches

*T*hen suddenly the glass was knocked over! It was the baby who'd kicked the glass over, all by itself. John shouted "Hooray!" but I thought the baby had spoiled Mom's shirt. Mom just laughed. She wasn't a bit angry. You can't be angry with someone who isn't even born yet, Mom said.

The good thing about my hair is that it doesn't hurt when it's combed. I know a girl who usually cries when her mother combs her hair. I like Mom to fix my hair. Sometimes she makes a ponytail, or ties a bow on it.

My doll, who's called Alice, has hair made of wool. So brushing her hair's quite hard, but I do it anyway. Having her hair brushed doesn't hurt Alice either. She looks best with pigtails, I think.

Before the baby is born, its whole body is covered with downy hair called lanugo. The lanugo falls off by the time the baby is born; only a little bit is left on the baby's head.

The white stuff on the baby's eyebrows is called vernix. It's like a natural wax that covers the whole baby while it is in the uterus. This protects the skin while the baby floats in the amniotic fluid.

Soon after the baby is born, the vernix is washed off.

6 months, 35 cm, 13½ inches

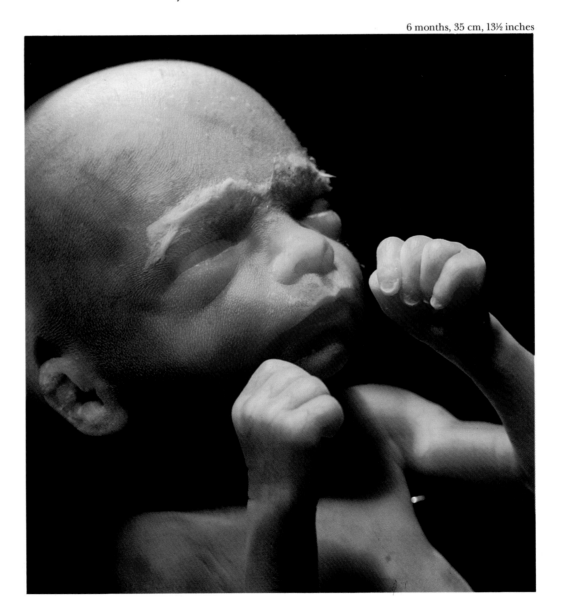

There are apples growing in our yard. First they're sour and small and green. Then they grow all summer, and they get red. They aren't ready to pick until I have to start wearing tights again. That's in the fall.

Sometimes we make apple cake and applesauce. They're good. I like ordinary apples off the tree, too, and I give a bite to Mom. When she eats I know the baby gets a taste too.

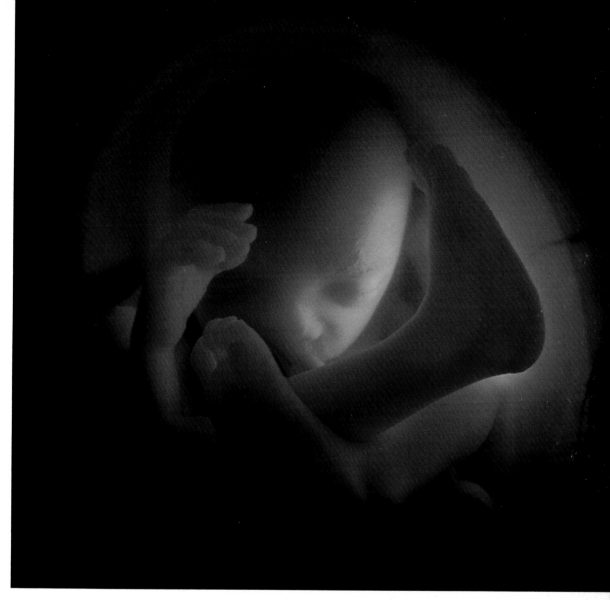

7 months, 40 cm, 15½ inches

Now the baby is like a real baby. Seven months have gone by since the sperm dug its way into the egg and the baby started growing. If the baby were born now, it would be able to live. But it would be as skinny and light as a little chicken. When the baby stays in the uterus longer, it gets plumper.

The lungs get stronger too. They are not used until the baby is born, because inside the uterus the baby doesn't need to breathe for itself. In there the baby gets all its oxygen through the umbilical cord.

*T*he best kind of secret house is up in a tree, I think. The tree doesn't have to be all that tall, of course.

   This is us at the tree house in the woods. I wanted to climb up into the tree house with John. But my legs didn't want to nearly as much. I wanted to climb higher up the ladder, but my legs wanted to take me down all the time.

   John said I was a sissy. But I wasn't. It was just my legs that wouldn't do what I wanted.

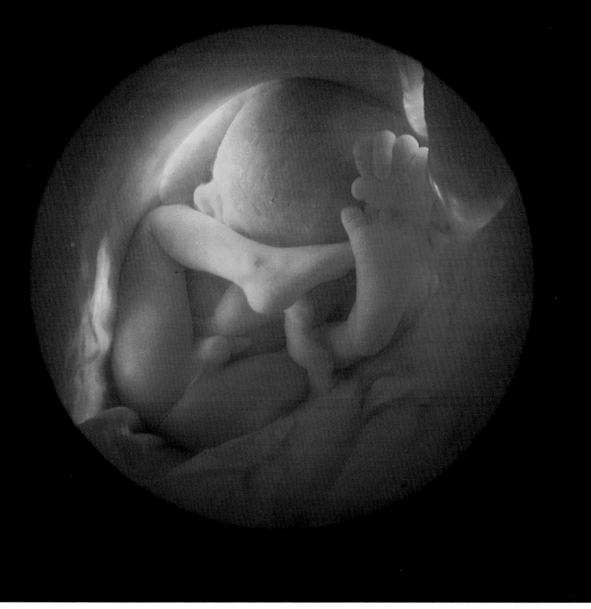

8 months, 45 cm, 17½ inches

Inside the mother's belly where the baby lies, it's like a secret house.
The baby's grown so big now that all it can do is lie still and kick.

The baby usually turns upside down in the end, since its head is
heaviest. Babies get born more easily if they come headfirst.

While it grows, the baby practices swallowing. It takes a sip of
amniotic fluid sometimes. The baby also pees. It doesn't matter;
nothing inside the uterus is dangerous for the baby.

At *the clinic they let us listen to our hearts on loudspeakers. John's heart sounded like "thump, thump." Mine was just like this: "crash, boom."*

The baby in Mom's tummy had a heart that sounded like a little watch. It ticked so fast. I laughed when I heard my own heart; it sounded so loud!

When I heard the baby's heart I thought it must be a little sister. That's good, because then her middle name could be Emma, just like mine is.

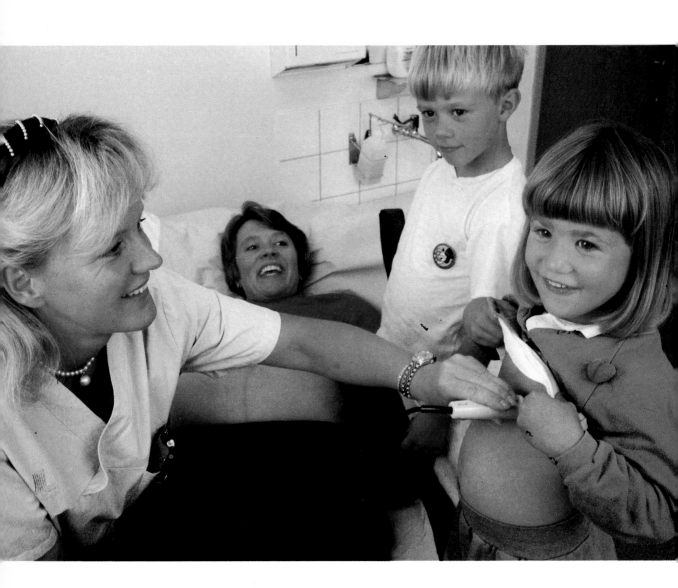

The baby's heart beats about 140 times a minute. That's twice as fast as the mother's own heart.

Now the mother's belly is very big. You can tell that there's a whole baby inside, kicking its feet and waving its fists. If a kick happens to land on the mother's bladder, she may almost wet herself—the baby kicks so hard.

The baby must be born soon. The mother's belly can't keep on stretching.

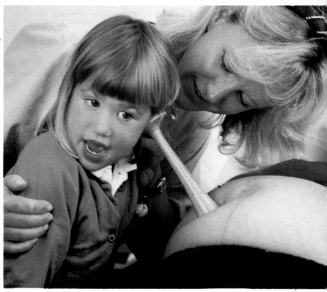

When I grow up I'm going to have a couch in my house. A red couch where I can curl up and read.

Sometimes in the evening when I can't sleep, I go to Mom and Daddy. They sit and talk a bit, and Mom has her legs up on the couch because that makes them feel better.

I want to sit on Mom's lap. But Mom says the baby's already on her lap and taking up all the room. I sit next to Mom instead, between her legs and the pillows, because there's room for that on a couch.

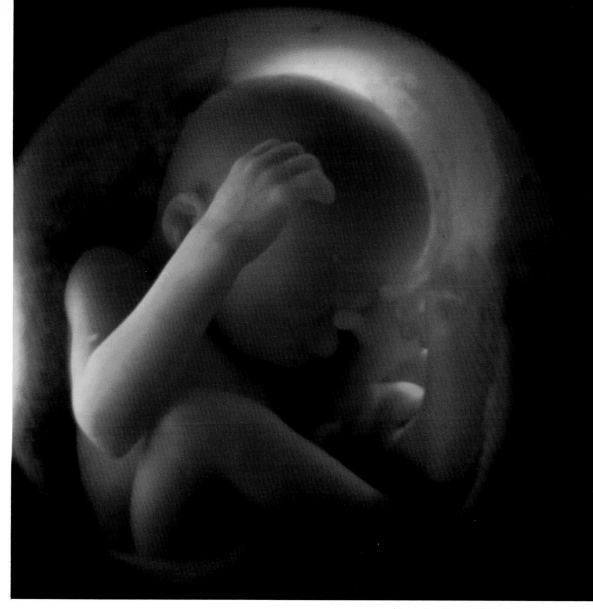

7 months, 40 cm, 15½ inches

The baby is resting, too, just like its mother. There's so little room left that all the baby can do is push and wiggle. It's crowded in there.

Now you can tell more about the baby. Some mothers have babies that kick a lot inside them. Others have babies that are quiet and seem to sleep most of the time.

The baby can hear well if you talk to it, and people think that it can learn to recognize voices through the belly wall. If a sound is sudden or loud and shrill, the baby gets frightened and gives a start.

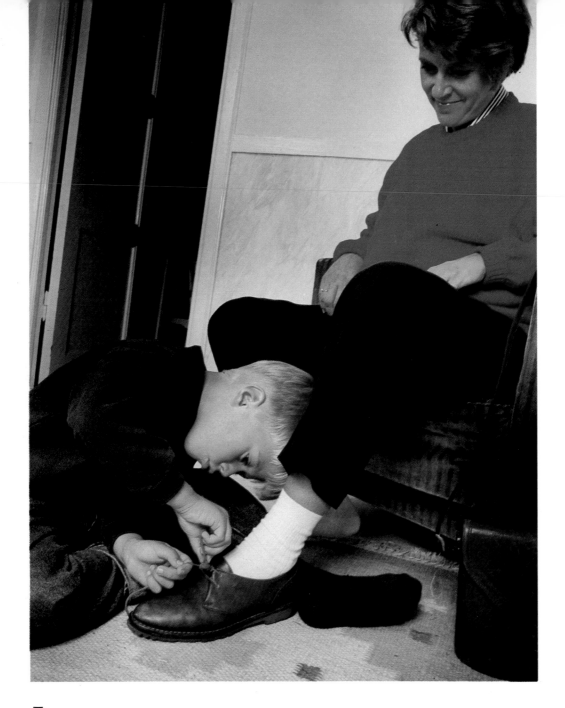

I'*ve noticed something about tummies. When people are fat all over, their tummies get soft and flabby. But when a mother's going to have a baby, her tummy gets smooth and quite hard.*

John can tie his shoelaces, almost. He helps Mom tie hers, because she keeps saying that her big tummy gets in the way when she wants to bend down.

*M*y Grandma thinks it's funny that such tiny socks used to fit me, *because I'm so big now. She and I looked at all the clothes the baby's going to wear when it's born. Some fit my doll Alice perfectly.*

Grandma let me choose pajamas for Alice. I chose some I'd had on when I was a baby. They were so cute and soft.

Mom said Grandma was going to be with us when the baby was born. I knew that was because Daddy was going to the hospital with Mom. But I didn't want her to go anyway.

Let's forget about the baby, I said to Mom. Two children are enough.

But Mom said we couldn't forget about the baby, because now it didn't have room in her tummy anymore. It wanted to be born now, no matter what.

Then I wanted to go, too, but they wouldn't let me. Grandma said we should get dinner ready. I was sad when Mom and Daddy left, because I didn't want my Mom to be in the hospital.

Now the baby wants to get out. The uterus keeps squeezing to help push out the baby. The squeezing is called contractions and the mother feels them more and more strongly. Contractions hurt, but not like stubbing your toe or having an earache. The way the mother feels is the special feeling of giving birth. It is called labor because it is hard work. The mother knows it's time to go to the hospital. She's packed her bag, and she's happy that the time has come.

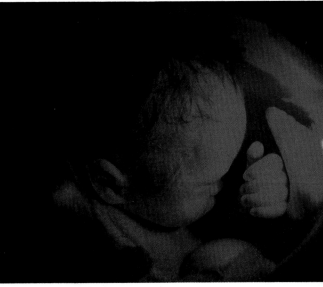

8½ months, 55 cm, 21½ inches

When a baby is born, it's called childbirth. Sometimes childbirth is quick; sometimes it takes many hours.

A doctor or nurse keeps checking to see how the mother and baby are feeling, since childbirth is such hard work. A mother must be strong to bring a baby into the world.

Every time the uterus squeezes, the baby is pushed down the vagina a bit more. Finally you see the top of its head between the mother's legs. Then it doesn't have far to go. Once the head is born, the rest of the body slides out like a small, slippery fish.

The baby starts breathing right after being born, and soon can start feeding from the mother's breasts. So now the umbilical cord is no longer needed. The doctor cuts the cord, which doesn't hurt the baby.

Our baby is a boy. We call him Thomas.

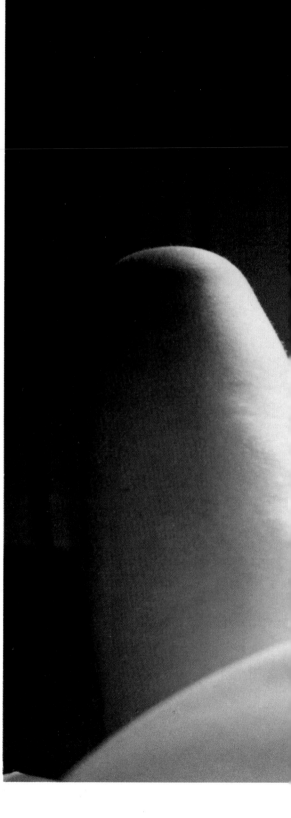

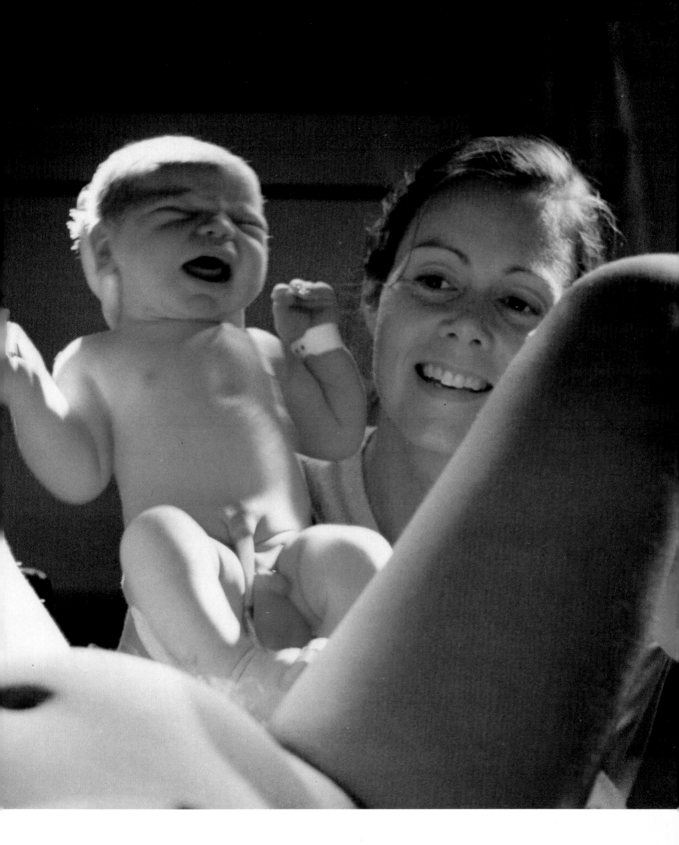

Right after being born, a newborn baby is usually wide awake, and not at all tired. That's just what Thomas is like too.

He lies in his mother's arms and looks around a bit. He breathes air and, for the first time, he sucks on his mother's breasts. This is good for the baby and for the mother too. Mothers and fathers like to have a quiet, happy time alone with their newborn baby.

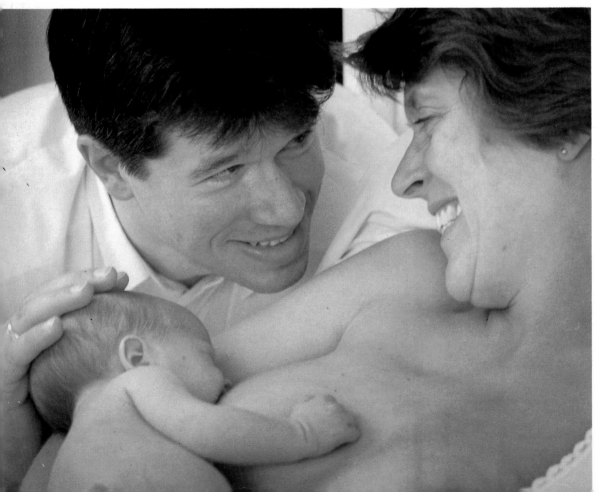

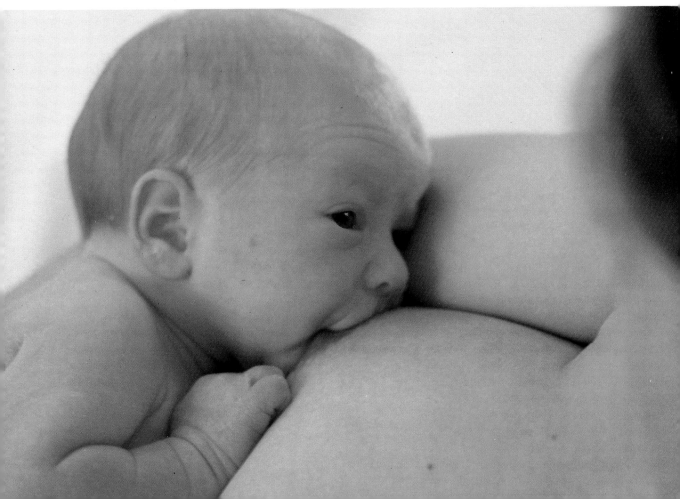

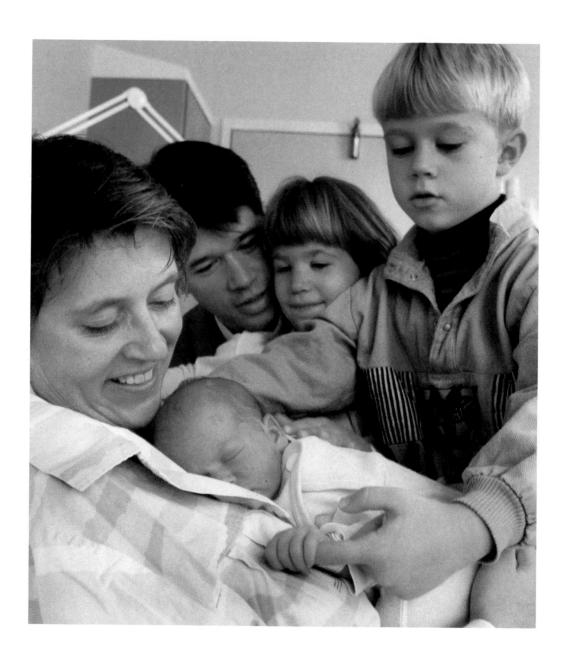

*W*hen Thomas was one day old, we went to the hospital with Daddy. Mom looked so happy when we got there. But I like it better when she has ordinary clothes on. I felt shy with Mom, because she didn't look like she usually does.

Thomas was so tiny! I thought he was cute and his head was warm when I kissed it.

Then I got to hold Thomas before John, because I asked first. It was hard, because a newborn baby is floppy. Thomas lay still on my lap and I looked at his hands. They were red and wrinkly, and his nails were the smallest I ever saw.

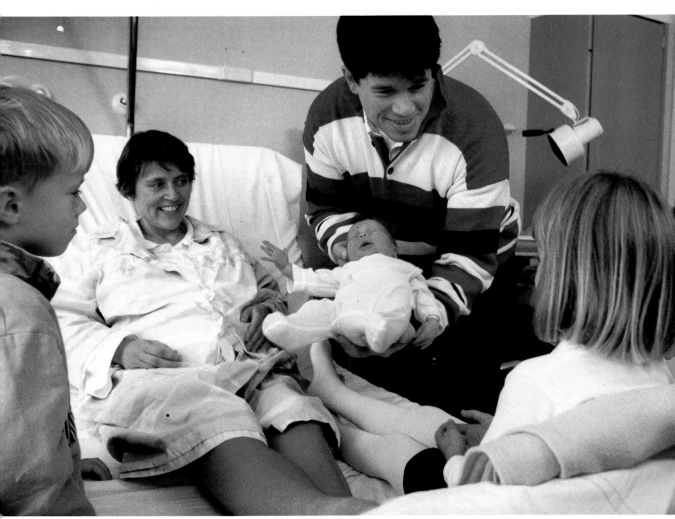

I helped Daddy to dress Thomas. Then I realized he can't have Emma as a middle name, because he's a boy. I didn't know that yesterday.

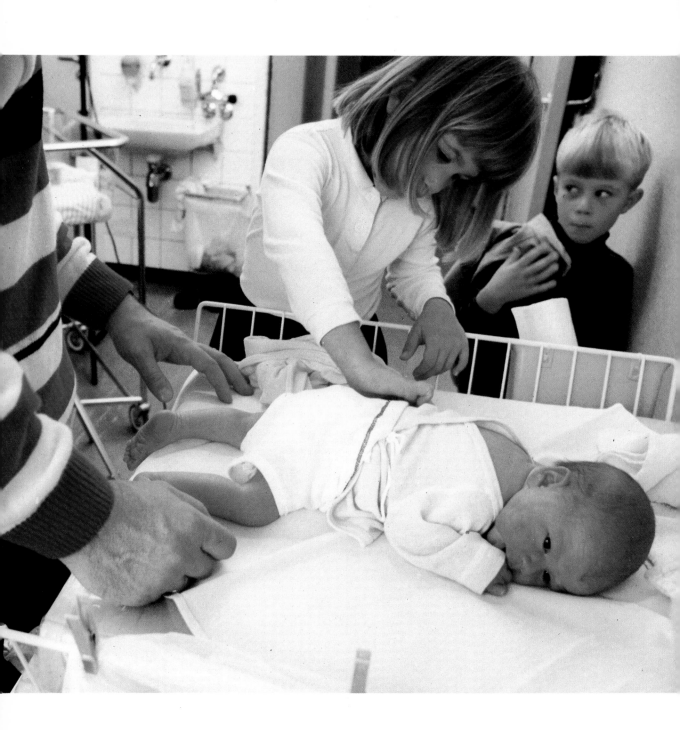

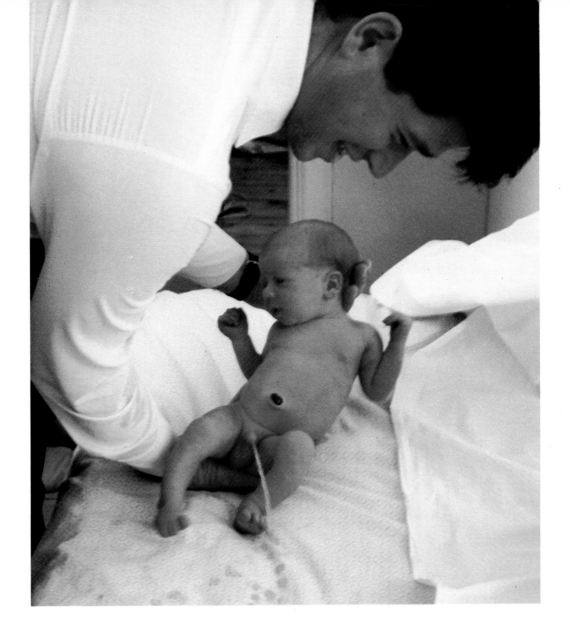

*Y*ou can see the little bit of umbilical cord left on Thomas. Mom said it was like that on all newborn babies and would soon fall off. I thought it was disgusting. It did fall off later, luckily, and he got a belly button just like mine.

Once when Daddy was changing his diaper Thomas started to pee, straight up in the air, like a fountain. We all laughed; it looked so funny.

Thomas didn't notice anything. He can't laugh yet. All he can do is sleep and eat and sleep and eat. And pee, of course.

Thomas grew so fast. He got to be a real fatso. Every time John and I talked with Thomas he started laughing and his little tummy jiggled. Mom said Thomas is sociable. You could see that.

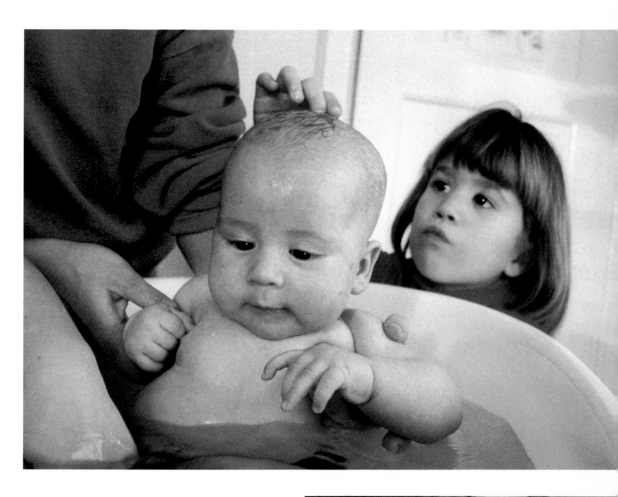

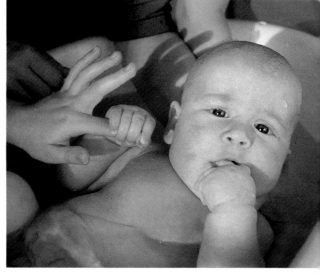

*T*homas can hold my finger hard. He's really strong! Mom says it's called the grasp reflex. All newborn babies can hold as strongly as that, but they don't know that they're doing it.

I like to help when Thomas has a bath. He's so smooth and soft, but he is slippery to hold when he's wet.

*L*ast Christmas there was no Thomas, but now there is. It's funny to think about.

Anyway, I can't remember what it was like before he came along. It feels as if we've always been a family with a Thomas in it.

When Daddy and John and I went to get the Christmas tree, I thought of something. It was that I'm both a little sister and a big sister now.

But John's just a big brother. And Thomas is just a little brother. So it's best being in the middle, like me.

*T*homas seems to get all the attention.

   When Mom and John fetch me from preschool, all the kids come and look at Thomas, even though Mom brings him almost every day. Once a girl called Ella jumped down from the top of the jungle gym just because she saw Mom coming with the baby carriage. She wanted to be the first of all the kids to look at Thomas—she sure is crazy! And our neighbor, who's name is Yoko, always wants to say hello to Thomas even though she has two kids herself.

   "But I don't have a baby anymore," Yoko says, and laughs.

*O*ur whole family loves Thomas so much. He's so happy and he's soft to hold and he can nearly stand up by himself. I've saved some socks that have already gotten too small for Thomas, because of something Grandma said. She told me that when I grow up, I'll probably have a baby of my own.

I've decided something.

It's that my baby's going to have Emma as her middle name.